Cameos of Christ

in the lives of some
Old Testament Characters

I0164324

Vicky Wilkinson

ISBN: 978-1-78364-465-0

The Open Bible Trust
Fordland Mount, Upper Basildon,
Reading, RG8 8LU, UK.

www.obt.org.uk

Cameos of Christ
in the lives of some
Old Testament Characters

Contents

Page

INTRODUCTION

INTRODUCTION

Sometime ago I attended a church Bible study during which we looked at the section of the Scriptures from Genesis to the end of Kings. As we looked into the lives of some of the Old Testament characters, we were struck with the many cameos of Christ Jesus portrayed in their lives. This should not be surprising because didn't Jesus Himself say to the Jews, "You search the Scriptures, for in them you think you have eternal life, and these are they which testify of ME" (John 5:39)? Jesus, of course, was referring to the Old Testament Scriptures in which we find not only manifold prophecies of Jesus Christ, but also a foreshadowing of His life and work in the lives of these Old Testament characters.

From the very time that things went wrong in the Garden of Eden, resulting in sin and death for the human race, God's pre-arranged plan to counteract this situation was immediately put into action. We find the first prophecy of a coming seed, who would eradicate sin and make possible the eventual fulfilment of God's original plan for the heavens and the earth, uttered in Genesis 3:15. This was addressed to the Serpent, whom we know to be Satan, who became the enemy of God and the root cause of sin and death. This seed is none other than the Lord Jesus Christ. God's plan and purpose to bring things back to His original plan is centred in and around Christ Jesus.

I have selected four of the early characters - Abraham - Joseph - Moses - Joshua, whom I will use as my examples and then to conclude I have briefly included King David and King Solomon. First though, I would like to point out that no man, however holy, can come anywhere near a full portrayal of the Lord Jesus. The reason being that all men, born since Adam, are under the curse of sin and death, and are therefore, imperfect (see Romans 5:12). In contrast, the Lord Jesus is holy and separate from sinners (Hebrews 7:26; 1 Peter 2:22). I hope you will be encouraged by these examples and see the need to study the Old Testament, as well as the New, to learn more about our Saviour.

ABRAHAM

ABRAHAM

The promised seed of Genesis 3:15 began with Adam and followed a line through his son Seth. It would have been Abel, except that Cain, Adam's firstborn, murdered him before he bore any children – Cain allowing himself to become the instrument of Satan in his attempt to destroy the line to the promised seed. However, God overruled in the birth of Seth (Genesis 4:25). The line to this seed is recorded in Genesis 5:1-32, 9:26, 11:10-26, bringing us to Abram (or Abraham as he became known as later). Not only was Abraham privileged to be in the line to Christ, but he was also chosen by God to become the father of a great nation, through which God would work out His plan and purpose for the earth. Why did God choose Abraham? We don't know. However, we could maybe look at the time when God chose David to be the king of Israel. On this occasion the Lord said to Samuel, "Do not look at his appearance or the height of his stature ... For the Lord does not see as man sees, for man looks at the outward appearance, but the Lord looks at the heart" (1 Samuel 16:7). Maybe the Lord saw something in the heart of Abraham that influenced His choice, for Abraham became the 'friend of God' (2 Chronicles 20:7; James 2:23).

Some of the cameos we find in Abraham's life are as follows:-

Abraham was obedient

Abraham was one of the prominent characters who received a mention in Hebrews 11, which is a chapter devoted to people of outstanding faith. Verse 8 says, "By faith Abraham obeyed when he was called to go out to the place which he would afterward receive as an inheritance. And he went out, not knowing where he was going." Here we note obedience, as well as faithfulness, was attributed to him.

Genesis 12:1-3 says:

> Now the Lord **had** said to Abram (as he was then named), "Get out of your country,

from your kindred, and from your father's house, to a land that I will show you. I will make you a great nation. I will bless you and make your name great and you shall be a blessing. I will bless those who bless you and I will curse him who curses you. And in you all the families on the earth shall be blessed."

If we backtrack a few verses to Chapter 11:26-32, we read of Abram's birth and early days, and that he obeyed God's command by leaving behind the comforts of the land of his birth. That he did receive his vision of God whilst he was in the land of Ur of Chaldeans is confirmed for us in Stephen's address or defence (see Acts 7:2-4).

However, returning to Genesis 11, it does say that Terah, his father, instigated the trip. Maybe as patriotic head of the family, Terah took over. Therefore Abram, along with his wife Sarai, his father Terah, and his nephew Lot, set off to go to the land which God would show them. However, when they came to Haran it says they dwelt there. Why they stopped there, we are not told.

Maybe Abraham's father had been taken ill and was unable to travel because it tells us that Terah died there. Another reason could have been that God had not intended Abram's father to be included in His plans. We just don't know.

After the death of his father, Abram, Sarai and Lot continued their journey until they came to the land of Canaan. That Abram had enjoyed a life of wealth and power in Ur, the land of his birth, is suggested by what we read in Genesis 13. It tells us that Abraham was very rich in livestock, silver and gold. These were probably the possessions they had gathered from Ur and Haran and had taken with them into Canaan. Both Abraham and Lot had herdsmen working under them in Canaan. These were probably the people they had acquired in Haran (12:5).

Christ Jesus was obedient

In a similar but even much greater way, at God's command or sending, the Lord Jesus willingly and obediently left behind the glories of His heavenly abode to go on a much greater journey

– from the great heavenly realms all the way down to the earth, to do His Father's will. His destination was the land of Israel (originally Canaan). Jesus said to the people, "For I have come down from heaven, not to do my own will, but the will of Him who sent me" (John 6:38). Verse 39 tells us that it was the Father who sent Him.

Like Abraham, Christ was called by God and sent to Canaan. Later in His ministry, Jesus referred back to the glories of His previous existence that He enjoyed with His Father in the heavens (see John 17:5).

Unlike Abraham who took with him some of his treasures to the new land, Christ not only left behind such glories, but He also emptied Himself or laid aside the outward attributes of His Deity when He came to the earth as a man, or be it a servant. When we read of this in Philippians 2:5-7, it says that He (Christ) didn't consider such things to be held on to, but was willing to let them go to become a servant, to accomplish God's will.

Abram flees to Egypt

In Abram's early days in Canaan there was a very severe famine in the land so he departed into Egypt to save the life of himself, his wife Sarai and all who accompanied him. Later Abram returned to Canaan (Israel) (Genesis 12:10; 13:1-5).

Jesus flees to Egypt

After being warned by an angel in a dream, Joseph takes his wife Mary and the young child, Jesus, into Egypt to save His life from the threat of Herod. After the death of Herod, Jesus returns to Israel with Mary and Joseph (Matthew 2:13 & 19-23).

Abram becomes man's intercessor

When Abram returned to Canaan after being in Egypt, it was mutually decided that he and Lot would separate (see Genesis 13:1-9). Abram gave Lot the choice of whether to go left or right. Lot chose for himself the Plain of Jordan, which included the City of Sodom, because it was well-watered everywhere and Abram took the opposite direction.

However, whilst the land which Lot had chosen was indeed beautiful, like the Garden of the Lord, even so the men of the city of Sodom were exceedingly wicked. In the course of time the outcry of the wickedness of Sodom, and its neighbour Gomorrah, rose up to the Lord and He came down to see for Himself if this was so. This was when the Lord appeared again to Abraham (the Lord having now changed his name from Abram at His last appearance). But this time it was at Mamre and renewed His promise to him of an heir by his wife Sarah (Genesis 18:1-15).

Before leaving, the Lord revealed to Abraham Sodom and Gomorrah's impending fate (Genesis 18:16-17). This was when Abraham humbly took upon himself the role of an intercessor and pleaded with the Lord for the people of Sodom, asking the Lord should fifty righteous be found in the cities would he spare them, and God said that He would. Five times more Abraham dared to plead with the Lord, the Judge of the earth, until he had narrowed it down to ten righteous men and each time the Lord agreed (Genesis 18:23-33). However, none were found to be righteous except Lot and his family who were spared by being led out by the angels.

Christ Jesus becomes man's intercessor

Even before Christ came down to the earth as the man Jesus, it was prophesied in Old Testament Scripture that He would become man's intercessor. In the well-known prophecy of the Suffering Servant in Isaiah 53, who without doubt is Christ Jesus, the Messiah, verse 12 says that He would make intercession for the transgressors. This He did when at His death, He was led as a lamb to the slaughter and the Lord laid on Him the iniquity of us all (Isaiah 53:6-7). Even at this traumatic time, Christ, as He hung on the Cross at Calvary, pleaded with the Father to forgive His crucifiers (Luke 23:34).

At the introduction of the section covering the Suffering Servant (Isaiah 52:13), it speaks of His exaltation and His being lifted on high. It was not possible that He would be held in death because again, it had been prophesied that the Father would not leave His soul in Hades (grave), nor would His Holy One see corruption (Psalm 16:9-11). Christ was raised up and exalted to the right hand of God, where He continued His role of intercessor. Hebrews 7:25 says, "Therefore, He is able also to save to the utmost those who come to God through Him, since He ever lives to make intercession for them." Whilst Abraham interceded for the people of Sodom and Gomorrah, Christ intercedes for all who come to Him.

An outstanding act of Abraham's faith

Abraham gets a second mention in the faith Chapter of Hebrews 11. Verses 17-19 say the following:

> By faith Abraham, when he was tested, offered up Isaac and he who received the promises offered up his only begotten son, of whom it was said, 'In Isaac your seed

shall be called', accounting that God was able to raise him up, even from the dead, from which he also received him in a figurative sense.

Genesis 22 records this extraordinary act of faith by Abraham which begins with a journey when God instructs him to take Isaac to a place called Moriah. To test Abraham, God tells him to take his only son, Isaac, and offer him as a burnt offering on a mountain there. Again Abraham obeyed God and did as He asked. He saddled his ass and along with Isaac and his young men and wood for the offering, he travelled to Moriah.

Can you imagine the pain and agony he suffered as he approached Moriah? Yet he still continued. When Isaac asked his father, "where is the lamb for the burnt offering?", Abraham answered, "God will provide for Himself a lamb." Although we know that God interceded and did not allow the sacrifice of Isaac to take place, Abraham's faith was so great that he believed that God would raise Isaac from the dead (Hebrews 11:17-19). He believed God's promise that in and through his son, Isaac, all families of the earth would be blessed (Genesis 12:2-3, 15:3-6). A ram caught in the thicket became a substitute offering. Therefore Abraham called the place 'Jehovah-jireh', which means 'The-Lord-will-provide'.

It is very interesting to note that Mount Moriah, the place God had designated for the burnt offering, was later the site of the city of Jerusalem and of Solomon's temple (see 2 Chronicles 3:1).

An outstanding act of Christ Jesus' faith

At the appointed time, Jesus took the twelve disciples aside and informed them of His intentions, which also began with a journey – a journey up to Jerusalem (previously the land of Moriah). He explained to them the reason behind this journey – although they did not seem to comprehend it at that time (Mark 10:32-33). Jesus entered Jerusalem riding on a colt of an ass along with His disciples, and the crowd greeted Him with "Hosanna! Blessed is He who comes in the name of the Lord!" (see Zechariah 9:9). However such cries soon turned to crucify Him! (Mark 15:13), and this they did. Jesus never faltered from His course of action. He willingly went on that journey that took Him to His death – death on the Cross of Calvary. This time there was no substitute ram. He became the Lamb that God provided – the Lamb of God who took away the sins of the world (John 1:29).

Abraham's outworking of faith involving his only begotten son to His wife Sarah, mirrored the great sacrificial offering of God through His only begotten Son, Jesus Christ - the true offering. Like Abraham, Christ reasoned or knew that God the Father would raise Him from the dead (Mark 10:34; Acts 3:15).

JOSEPH

JOSEPH

The line of the seed to Christ continued from Abraham through his son Isaac and his son Jacob.

Joseph, who was the eleventh son of Jacob, was not in the line to Christ, because this was continued through Jacob's fourth son Judah (which became the royal tribe). Even so, by the events which took place in his life, Joseph was chosen by God to save from extinction not only the royal line to the seed, but also the whole nation, which was also integral to the outworking of God's purpose.

I have to say that Joseph is one of my Old Testament favourites and the account of his life and character has found a special place in my heart. As far as I can see, out of all the Old Testament characters, there are more cameos of Jesus portrayed in the life of Joseph than in any of the others. Those that I have been able to pick up on are as follows:-

Joseph was especially beloved of his father

Jacob, whom God named Israel, especially loved Joseph above all his other children because he was the firstborn son of Rachel his beloved wife, and also the son of his old age. Jacob made Joseph a coat of many colours which made his brothers jealous of him (Genesis 37:3-4)

Christ Jesus was especially beloved of His Father

Jesus came to John and was baptised in the Jordan. Immediately, coming up from the water, John saw the heavens parting and the Spirit descended upon Jesus like a dove. Then a voice from heaven said: "You are My beloved Son, in whom I am well pleased" (Mark 1:9-11).

Joseph was hated by his own brethren

When Joseph's brothers saw that their father loved him more than them, they hated him and could not speak peaceably to him. And when Joseph related his dreams to them that indicated they would bow down to him, they hated him even more for his dreams and his words (Genesis 37:4).

Christ Jesus was hated by His own brethren

"He Came to His own but His own did not receive Him" (John 1:11). The Father sent His Son to first save His own people. Christ said, "I was not sent except to the lost sheep of the House of Israel" (Matthew 15:24). But the nation as a whole rejected Him and only a very few individuals accepted Him and recognised Him as the Messiah, the sent One. It was the leaders of the Jews that stirred the people against Him and sent Him to His death. It was His own people, the Jews, who cried, "Crucify Him, crucify Him" (Mark 15:11-14; Luke 23:20-21).

Joseph was betrayed for pieces of silver

Joseph's brothers went to Shechem to feed their father's flock there. Jacob sent Joseph to check on them, and see if all was well with them, and then to return and report back to him. Joseph eventually found his brothers in Dothan. When his brothers saw him coming to them in the distance, they conspired to kill him. But Reuben (the eldest of the brothers) persuaded them not to kill him but rather to cast him into a pit. (His plan was to return and save him later).

So they first stripped him of his coat of many colours and cast him into a pit. But unknown to Reuben, the other brothers saw some Ishmaelites approaching and decided to sell him as a slave for twenty pieces of silver. When Reuben returned to save him he was not there. He returned to his brothers in anguish and tore his clothes! He was very scared because being the eldest, he was responsible for him. Therefore, Joseph's brothers devised a scheme. They killed a kid of the goats, dipped Joseph's coat into its blood and took the coat home to Jacob, saying that they had found it. Assuming that Joseph must have been devoured by a wild beast, Jacob tore his clothes, put on sackcloth and mourned for his son. He refused to be comforted by his family and wept for Joseph (Genesis 37:12-36).

Christ Jesus was betrayed for pieces of silver

Joseph was betrayed by those very near to Him, his own brothers, and in a similar way, Jesus was betrayed by one very near to him - one of His disciples. It was Judas Iscariot, who had been with Him throughout His ministry, who betrayed Him (see Psalm 41:9). Jesus knew in advance of Judas' future betrayal (see John 6:70-71). Judas acted as treasurer on behalf of the disciples and Scripture indicates that Judas had already turned traitor when it named him as a thief (John 12:1-6). It was Judas himself who approached the chief priests and said, "What are you willing to give me if I deliver Him to you?" And they counted out thirty pieces of silver (Matthew 26:14-16).

It was at the feast of the Passover (the last supper) that Jesus spoke of His betrayer, saying, "Most assuredly, I say to you, one of you will betray Me" When the disciples asked "Who is it?", Jesus answered, "It is he to whom I shall give a piece of bread when I have dipped it." He then gave this dipped bread to Judas and said to him, "What you do, do it quickly." Judas left immediately – the other disciples assumed that because he held the money box, Jesus had sent him on an errand (John 13:21-30).

After the Passover supper, Jesus, and His disciples, went to the garden of Gethsemane to pray. Whilst they were there, a multitude with swords and clubs came from the chief priests led by Judas. Judas drew near to Jesus and kissed Him. Christ said, "Are you betraying the Son of Man with a kiss?" (Luke 22:48). They then took Jesus, bound Him and led Him away. When Judas realised the terrible thing he had done, he tried to return the money but the chief priests would not accept it, so he threw it in the temple, went away and hanged himself. The chief priests took the silver pieces and said, "it is not lawful to put them in the treasury, because it is the price of blood." Therefore with the thirty pieces of silver (the price of Christ's betrayal), they bought a potter's field to bury strangers in. This field became known as 'the field of blood' (Matthew 27:3-10 – compare Zechariah 11:12-13). Judas was later replaced by Matthias (Acts 1:23-26 – compare Psalm 109:7-8).

As a young person, Joseph was taken into Egypt

The Ishmaelites took Joseph into Egypt and they sold him to Potiphar, an officer of Pharaoh and captain of the guard. The Lord was with Joseph and he was successful in all he did in the house of his master, the Egyptian (Genesis 39:1-2).

As a young person, Jesus was taken into Egypt

Following the visit of the wise men from the east, an angel of the Lord appeared unto Joseph and said, "Arise, take the young child and his mother, flee to Egypt, and stay there until I bring you word; for Herod will seek the young child to destroy Him" (Matthew 2:13).

Joseph gave the glory and honour to God

When Pharaoh asked Joseph if he could interpret his dream, Joseph said, "It is not in me, God will give Pharaoh an answer" (Genesis 41:16). Joseph gave the glory and credit of his interpretation to God (see also verses 25-28).

Christ Jesus gave the glory and honour to God

Jesus always gave the glory and honour to God the Father for the Words He spoke and the works He did (John 14:10-13).

Joseph resisted temptation and was faithful in all things

Now Joseph was a very handsome man in both form and appearance and whilst he was in Potiphar's service, his master's wife lusted after him. However, Joseph, being a faithful man to God and to his master, refused her continuous invitations to lie with her and fled from her presence (Genesis 39:1-12).

Christ Jesus resisted temptation and was faithful in all things

The Holy Spirit led Jesus into the wilderness where He fasted for forty days and nights. The devil took the advantage because he knew He was hungry and tired. Three times the devil tried to tempt Jesus, but on each occasion He used the Word of God as His defence (Matthew 4:1-10). Jesus in His human form remained faithful to the Father in all things (Hebrews 2:17-18).

All things were placed into Joseph's hands.

Whilst in Potiphar's service, Joseph's master saw that the Lord was with him and all that he did prospered. Therefore, Potiphar made Joseph overseer of all his household and placed all things into his hand (Genesis 39:3-5).

When Joseph was unjustly put into prison, the Lord was with him and showed him mercy and gave him favour in the sight of the keeper of the prison. Therefore, the prison keeper committed to

Joseph's hand all the prisoners and the running of the prison (Genesis 39:20-23).

All things were placed into Christ Jesus' hands

As the feast of the Passover approached, Jesus knew His hour had come He knew that the Father had given all things into His hands, and that He had come from God and was going back to God (John 13:3).

Joseph was thirty years old when he began his ministry in Egypt

When Joseph had interpreted Pharaoh's dreams and advised him what to do, Pharaoh said to his servants, "can we find such a one as this, a man in whom is the Spirit of God?" Therefore, Pharaoh set Joseph to rule over his entire house and also over all the land of Egypt. Only his throne he withheld from Joseph. Pharaoh clothed him in fine garments, gave him his own personal signet ring and put a gold chain around his neck. He had him ride in the second chariot to himself and he gave his own daughter to be Joseph's wife. Joseph was thirty years old when he began his service to Pharaoh (Genesis 41:41-46).

Christ Jesus was about thirty years old when he began his ministry in Israel

Jesus began His ministry by being baptised by John the Baptist in the river Jordan. Jesus' baptism was not a baptism of repentance as it was for the Judean people (because Jesus was sinless) but rather a sign to John that He was the Son of God. John witnessed the Spirit descending from heaven like a dove, and remaining on Him. He also heard a voice from heaven say, "This is My Beloved Son, in whom I am well pleased" (John 1:29-33; Matthew 3:13-17). In Luke's genealogy of Jesus Christ, he tells us that Jesus was about the age of thirty years when He began his ministry (Luke 3:23).

Joseph forgave his brother's sin

When Joseph's brothers came a *second time* to Egypt to buy food because of the famine in Canaan, they brought Benjamin, the youngest brother, with them as stipulated by Joseph. It was on this visit that Joseph made himself known to his brothers. It was with great emotion that Joseph did this and the entire household heard him weep. At first Joseph's brothers were unnerved and scared until Joseph reassured them that he had forgiven them for what they had done to him. In fact he explained to them that what they did had been part of God's plan. He said, "And God sent me before you to preserve a posterity for you in the earth and to save your lives by a great deliverance" (Genesis 45:7; see also chapters 43 – 45).

Christ Jesus forgave His brother's sin

It was Jesus' own people who sent Him to His death. Christ was led to the place called Calvary and there they crucified Him. Whilst Christ was hanging on the Cross, Jesus said, "Father, forgive them, for they do not know what they do" (Luke 23:34). That Jesus had forgiven the Jews was demonstrated by the fact that the disciples of Jesus, after His death, continued their ministry to try and save this nation. After the disciples received the Holy Spirit, Peter addressed all the people of Israel and said to them:

> "Therefore, let all the house of Israel know assuredly that God has made this Jesus, whom you crucified, both Lord and Christ." Now when they heard this they were cut to the heart, and said to Peter, "What shall we do?" Then Peter said to them, "Repent, and let every one of you be baptised in the name of Jesus Christ for the remission of sins; and you shall receive the gift of the Holy Spirit" (Acts 2:36-38).

Sadly, this spirit of repentance didn't last and by the end of the Acts period, the people, as a nation, rejected Christ (Acts 28:17-29).

Another interesting parallel between Christ and Joseph is that it isn't until the *second time* that Christ reveals Himself to Israel. At His second coming, the Bible tells us, they will see and recognise their Saviour, the One whom they pierced, and they will repent with much mourning and weeping (Revelation 1:7; Zechariah 12:10-14).

Joseph was the Saviour of His people

All that happened to Joseph had been in the providence of God. Through Joseph and his ministry to Pharaoh in Egypt during the famine years, he saved not only the lives of the Egyptians but also the lives of his own family, which eventually became the Nation of Israel. Whilst the adversary of God plotted to destroy the forefathers of God's chosen people by famine in the land of Canaan, God was ahead of him by preparing a saviour through Joseph and his work in Egypt. Joseph's actions not only saved his own people but preserved the line to the special seed to come, who was to be the true Saviour.

Christ Jesus was the Saviour of His people

Throughout the Old Testament there had been the promise of a Saviour for God's people, and when we move on into the New Testament this promise became a reality at the birth of Jesus. The angel of the Lord announced to the shepherds living out in the fields, "For there is born to you this day in the city of David, a Saviour, who is Christ the Lord" (Luke 2:11).

The Apostle Paul when addressing the people at Antioch said, "From this man's (David's) seed, according to the promise, God raised up for Israel, a Saviour" (Acts 13:23). Through the line of King David, the Messiah came who was to save Israel. Whilst the whole nation at that time did not accept their Saviour, but rather sent Him to His death, Bible prophecy says that things will be different when Christ returns a second time. Paul said, when the fullness of the Gentiles has come in, then all Israel will be saved, as it is written, "The Deliverer will come out of Zion, and He will turn away ungodliness from Jacob, for this is my covenant with them, when I take away their sins" (Romans 11:25-27). The unconditional promises made to Israel must be fulfilled, as its says, "But Israel shall be saved by the Lord with an everlasting salvation (Isaiah 45:17).

Joseph's humiliation and subsequent exaltation

As a young person, Joseph held a prominent position within his family. As mentioned earlier, Joseph was the firstborn son to Jacob's beloved wife Rachel, who had spent many of her married years barren, but was then blessed by the Lord with two sons, Joseph and Benjamin. Therefore, when Joseph was born, he was much loved of his father and his mother – hence he was given the coat of many colours.

However, Joseph's young days of glory came to an abrupt end when he was sold by his jealous brothers as a slave and taken into Egypt. Joseph was sold on as a servant to Potiphar, an Officer of Pharaoh and captain of the guard. Now the Lord was with Joseph in Potiphar's service, and Joseph fared well until, yet again, Joseph was brought down unjustly and sent to prison.

Even though the Lord continued to be with Joseph and made him favourable with the prison keeper, still Joseph did not have his freedom and remained parted from his father and family and remained in prison for several years. Whilst in prison, Joseph had correctly interpreted the dreams of the chief butler and the chief baker of Pharaoh, who were also in prison, and this came to light some years later when Pharaoh had two dreams that had greatly disturbed him. It was then that the chief butler remembered Joseph and recommended him to Pharaoh.

God, through Joseph, had been able to interpret the disturbing dreams of Pharaoh and as a reward Joseph was set free from prison and Pharaoh made Joseph his right hand man. Pharaoh set Joseph over all the land of Egypt to prepare for the years of famine whilst they had the years of plenty. When Joseph's brothers came to Egypt to buy food in the famine years, they bowed down before him, as he said they would in his dream as a young boy (Genesis 37:5-11; 43:28). Therefore, Joseph, in his lifetime, was brought down in humiliation but rose up again to exaltation.

Christic Jesus' humiliation and subsequent exaltation

Philippians Chapter 2:1-11 points us to Christ Jesus as the perfect example of one with humility. Before Christ came down to the earth, He existed in the glorious heavenly realms in the form of God (This means He possessed all the attributes of God). But these verses tell us that He was willing to leave behind and divest Himself of such glories, and come down to this earth as the man Jesus, even a Servant. Jesus said to the Jews, to whom He was sent, "I am the living bread which came down from heaven" (John 6:51). Christ Jesus was sent down to this earth to do His Father's will (John 6:38) and He was obedient in every way, even to the point of death – the death of the Cross. This was why He came to give His life for man's sin, in order that we can have hope.

Because of this, God has highly exalted Him to a place at His own right hand in the higher heavenlies, and also given Him a name which is above every name, that at the name of Jesus, every knee should bow, in heaven and the earth and under the earth, and every tongue confess that Jesus Christ is Lord, to the glory of God the Father. God the Father has given Him back the glory He had with Him before the world was (John 17:5).

MOSES

MOSES

The life story of Joseph explains how the Israelites came to be in the land of Egypt. From Jacob (the father of Joseph) and his twelve sons came the Israelite nation. When the Pharaoh who had known Joseph died and another took his place, the children of Israel increased and multiplied and became so mighty that they filled the land.

The new Pharaoh was afraid they would overtake the Egyptians, so he set taskmasters over them to afflict them, and this is where Moses appeared on the scene and was used by God to set His people free from their slavery. God's intention was to deliver them back to the land He had promised to them through Abraham, Isaac and Jacob.

Some cameos of Jesus that occurred in the life of Moses were as follows:-

As a young child Moses was preserved from death

A married couple from the Tribe of Levi had a son who was very beautiful. However, the Pharaoh had commanded that all male babies born to the Hebrew women should be thrown into the river. I think most people know the Bible account of Moses in the bulrushes. To try and save him from death, his mother made a cradle of bulrushes, which she waterproofed, laid her baby in, and put it amongst the reeds by the river bank.

The child was found by the daughter of Pharaoh and when she saw how beautiful he was, she had compassion on him, and he became her son and she named him Moses (which means *saved from water*) (Exodus 2).

As a young child Jesus was preserved from death

Following the visitation of the wise from the east, who came to worship the One who had been born King of the Jews, an angel appeared to Joseph in a dream, telling him to arise and take the young child into Egypt, because king Herod was out to destroy the young child. So Joseph took the young child, Jesus and His mother, Mary, into Egypt and they stayed there until the death of Herod (Matthew 2:13-18).

Moses controlled the sea

Following the ten plagues that God had brought upon the people of Egypt, the Pharaoh eventually gave in and allowed Moses to lead his people out of Egypt. After the Israelites had fled, Pharaoh once again hardened his heart and made the decision to pursue them.

By this time God's people had been led by the Lord and had set up camp at Pi Hahiroth opposite Baal Zephon by the Red Sea. When the people saw the Egyptians pursuing them on horses and riding chariots, they were so afraid for they had no escape with only the sea in front of them, so they began to wish they were back in Egypt.

On hearing their lament, Moses stood before the people and said, "Do not be afraid, stand still and see the salvation of the Lord. The Lord will fight for you and you will hold your peace" (Exodus 14:14).

First, with the Pillar of Cloud, the Angel of the Lord went before them to lead them and also went behind them. The cloud gave light to the Children of Israel, but only darkness to the pursuing Egyptians. Then Moses stretched out his hand over the sea and the Lord caused the sea to be divided, creating a wall of water on each side, and God's people crossed on dry ground in the midst of the sea.

The Egyptians pursued them into the sea, but when the children of Israel had all crossed over, the Lord instructed Moses to once again stretch his hand out over the sea and the waters returned to their normal depths, drowning the pursuing Egyptians, horsemen and their chariots. So the Lord saved Israel that day by the hand of Moses and the people sang a song of deliverance (Exodus 14 – 15).

Christ Jesus controlled the sea

Following the Sermon on the Mount, the crowds pursued Jesus and His disciples, so Jesus commanded that they cross over to the other side of the Sea of Galilee. They climbed into the boat and set off for the other side and Jesus fell asleep. But suddenly a great storm arose so that waves were cascading into the boat but Jesus slept on. The disciples woke Him and cried, "Lord save us, we are perishing." Jesus said to them, "why are you fearful, O you of little faith." Then He arose and rebuked the winds and the sea and there was a great calm. His disciples marvelled and said, "Who can this be, that even the winds and the sea obey Him?" (Matthew 8:18-27).

Moses fasted for forty days and forty nights

The Lord summoned Moses to cut two tablets of stone, go up Mount Sinai and there appear in His presence on the top of the mountain. Then the Lord descended in a cloud, stood with Moses, and proclaimed the name of the Lord. As well as writing the Law on tablets of stone, the Lord renewed His covenant with the people. So Moses was there in the presence of the Lord forty days and forty nights during which he neither ate bread or drank water (Exodus 34:1-28).

Christ Jesus fasted for forty days and forty nights

Following His baptism by John the Baptist, Jesus, being filled with the Holy Spirit, was led by the Spirit into the wilderness, being tempted for forty days by the devil. During that time Jesus ate nothing and afterwards He was hungry (Luke 4:1-2).

Moses' face shone from God's Glory

When Moses had come down from the mount carrying the tablets of the testimony, the skin of his face shone from being in the presence of the glory of God and the people were afraid to come near him. Therefore, Moses put a veil over his face. However, when he went in before the Lord to speak with Him, he took off the veil. When he came out he put the veil back on and then would speak to the children of Israel all the words of the Lord that he had been commanded (Exodus 34:29-35).

And, concerning the people of Israel of his day, Paul wrote that "Even to this day, when Moses is read, a veil covers their hearts", because their hearts remained hardened towards Christ (2 Corinthians 3:13-16).

Christ Jesus' face shone from God's glory

Jesus took Peter, James and John up on a high mountain and was transfigured before them. His face shone like the sun and His clothes became as white as the light. And behold Moses and Elijah appeared to them, talking with Him. Peter asked if he could make three tabernacles, one for Jesus, one for Moses and one for Elijah. But while Peter was still speaking, a bright cloud overshadowed them and suddenly a voice came out of the cloud saying, "This is my Beloved Son in whom I am well pleased. Hear Him!" (Matthew 17:1-8).

2 Corinthians 3:7-18 makes the contrast between the glory connected with the Old Covenant, which caused the face of Moses to shine, resulting in him veiling his face, and the glory of the Lord, which true believers can behold unveiled, because the veil is taken away in Christ.

Moses appointed seventy helpers

Whilst on their wilderness travels, the Lord provided manna for the children of Israel, which the people gathered daily, except on the Sabbath. They ground it, cooked it in pans, and made cakes of it which tasted like pastry prepared with oil. But the people grumbled and wept and asked Moses for meat. Moses entreated the Lord and said, "I am not able to bear all these people alone because the burden is too heavy for me." So the Lord told Moses to select seventy men of the elders of the people and bring them to the Tabernacle of Meeting so they could stand there with Moses. The Lord continued, "I will take of the Spirit that is upon you and put the same upon them, and they shall bear the burden of the people with you, so that you may not bear it yourself alone." So Moses did as the Lord instructed and when the Spirit of God rested on the selected men, they prophesied (Numbers 11).

Christ Jesus appointed seventy helpers

As well as appointing twelve apostles to aid Him in His ministry, Jesus also appointed a further seventy helpers. He sent them out two by two into each city and place, in preparation for His visit to them. He said to them, "The harvest truly is great, but the labourers are few; therefore pray the Lord of the harvest to send out labourers into His harvest." He gave them careful instructions of what they should do and what they should not do. They returned with joy and said, "Lord, even the demons are subject to us in your name" (Luke 10:1-22).

Moses became man's mediator

When Moses brought the people out of the camp to meet with God, they stood at the foot of Mount Sinai. They were not allowed to touch the mountain, lest they die. The Lord descended upon the mount in a fire, its smoke ascended like the smoke of a furnace, and the whole mountain shook, and the people were very afraid. And when the blast of the trumpet sounded long and became louder and louder, Moses spoke and God answered him by voice (Exodus 19).

The people were so afraid that they asked Moses to mediate God's words to them for they were afraid that they would die. So from that day onwards when Moses met with God, he then brought God's words to His people. He became the mediator between God and the children of Israel. He spoke to them all the Law and commandments of the Lord (Exodus 20:18-19; 21:1).

Christ Jesus became man's mediator

Hebrews chapter 12 speaks of the above occasion when God ascended on Mount Sinai in fire, darkness and tempest, and the people were very afraid including Moses. It then contrasts it with Mount Zion, the city of the living God, the heavenly Jerusalem. As Moses was the mediator of the old covenant that was given with the sprinkling of blood (see Exodus 24:7-8), Jesus is the mediator of the new covenant, that gives the promise of a better hope, a heavenly city, which was validated by His own shed blood at Calvary (Hebrews 9:15).

Not only is Christ Jesus the mediator of the New Covenant, but He is also the mediator between God and all men. "For there is one God and one mediator between God and men, the Man Christ Jesus, who gave Himself a ransom for all" (1 Timothy 2:5-6). Christ is now risen and ascended and sits at the right hand of God as our mediator and intercessor. Whatever we ask of God, Jesus said that we should ask it in His name.

God's people were baptised into Moses

1 Corinthians 10:1-2 says,

> Moreover, brethren, I do not want you to be unaware that all our fathers were under the cloud, all passed through the sea, all were

baptised into Moses in the cloud and in the sea.

The Children of Israel, by their obedience to God's instructions through Moses, by putting the blood of the Passover lamb on their lintels resulting in the saving of their lives, and by crossing the Red sea under the Cloud on dry ground, experienced a kind of redemption and a baptism into Moses. This wasn't a baptism with water, but a dry baptism – the people never even got wet. When they were safely across, and Moses stretched his hand out over the sea, God caused the waters to return, drowning the pursuing Egyptians. Then the people sang to the Lord, "The Lord is my strength and song, He has become my salvation" (Exodus 15:2).

God's people are baptised into Christ Jesus

The above baptism of the children of Israel as they passed through the sea on dry ground was a picture or anti-type of a spiritual baptism into Christ. The Apostle Paul said to the Christians at Rome:

Or do you not know that as many of us as were baptised into Christ, were baptised into His death? Therefore we were buried with Him through baptism into death, that just as Christ was raised from the dead by the glory of the Father, even so we should walk in the newness of life. For if we have been united together in the likeness of His death, certainly we shall also be in the likeness of His resurrection. (Romans 6:3-5).

This is applicable to a spiritual baptism into the death of Christ. By belief or faith in Christ's work of redemption, we died with Him (that is our old nature along with its sin), we were buried with Him, and we were also raised up to the newness of life, as a new creation in Christ. Therefore, we should reckon ourselves dead to sin, but alive to God in Christ Jesus our Lord (v.11).

JOSHUA, DAVID AND SOLOMON

The last three Old Testament characters I would like us to consider are Joshua, David and Solomon. In the lives of these three men we see cameos with a difference. They are all applicable to the future, when Christ returns to first gather His people, brings them to their inheritance, and sets up His throne and kingdom. Therefore, these cameos give us foresight of future events to come as promised or foretold in the Scriptures.

JOSHUA

JOSHUA

During the forty years that the Israelites wandered in the desert, the first generation that came out of Egypt gradually died off and only their offspring was left. That is with the exception of Joshua, the son of Nun, and Caleb. Their lives had been preserved because they had been especially faithful to the Lord when God sent men to spy out the land, when they first came to the borders of Canaan (read Numbers 13 and 14, 26:63-65). Therefore, following the death of Moses, the Lord appointed Joshua to take the place of Moses and lead the new generation on to their inheritance, the land flowing with milk and honey, which the Lord had promised them. Therefore, whilst Moses was instrumental in the salvation or redemption of the nation, it was Joshua whom God used to take the nation on to their inheritance.

Whilst the Promised Land was the inheritance that God's people were brought to at that time, when we read Hebrews 11, we see that God had an even greater inheritance in store for the faithful. In this chapter of Hebrews, this inheritance is described as being a better inheritance or country that was attached to a better resurrection (Hebrews 11:16,35,40). It tells us that all those great men and women of faith did not receive it in their lifetime but it was future.

To receive their inheritance, God's people, lead by Joshua, must first cross over Jordan

The Lord was with Joshua, as He was with Moses, and Joshua gathered the people from their desert wanderings and brought them to the edge of the River Jordan. To receive their inheritance, God's people must first cross over the Jordan and it was here that the Lord mirrored what He did forty years earlier at the Red Sea. The Lord cut off the waters that came from upstream, so that they stood in a heap As a result the Israelites, led by the Ark of the Covenant, were able to cross the Jordan on dry ground (Joshua 3:14-17). We could say this second generation of Israelites experienced a baptism into Joshua, whose name means *Jah is Salvation.*

To receive their inheritance, all believers of Jesus Christ must first cross over

As the Israelites received a kind of baptism when they crossed the Red Sea and the River Jordan, all believers today who have put their faith in Christ Jesus, receive a baptism into Christ Jesus. Romans 6:3-4 says:

> Or do you not know that as many of us who were baptised into Christ Jesus, were baptised into His death? Therefore we were buried with Him through baptism into His death.

Christ died for our sins and He took them with Him to the grave. From a spiritual viewpoint, in faith we also died and were buried with Him, to loose us from our sins. Through God's grace and faith we stand in Christ's righteousness. However, from a literal viewpoint we still have our body of flesh along with its sinful nature. At this side of Jordan, our old nature and our new nature dwell together side by side! To rid ourselves of our sinful body and go on into our inheritance, we must first cross over from death into life and this will be our crossing over Jordan. We will also have to sleep awhile in Jesus until the time of Christ's second coming or His appearance, to take us home to glory – whether it be on the earth, in the New Jerusalem or in the higher heavens (Philippians 3:20-21; 1 Thessalonians 4:13-14).

Joshua said that not all would have to cross over

As Joshua prepared his people to cross the River Jordan, he said to the Reubenites, the Gadites and the half-tribe of Manasseh, that their wives and children were to stay on this side of the river. Their inheritance was on this side of Jordan, but the mighty men of valour must first cross over to help the other tribes to take their possession, then they could return to their families (Joshua 1:12-15; 22:1-4).

Christ Jesus said not all would have to cross over

Jesus said, "I am the resurrection and the life. He who believes in me, though he may die, he shall live. And whoever lives and believes in me shall never die ..." (John 11:25-26). Jesus indicated that there were some who would not need to cross over (die) and this is also confirmed for us in 1 Thessalonians 4:13-17. When the Lord descends from heaven at His coming, He will bring with Him those who sleep in Jesus, and those believers who are still alive at that time will be translated or changed (see also 1 Corinthians 15:51-52).

Joshua heralds his coming

When the people of Jericho saw that the army of Israel approached their city, and heard what the Lord had done for them at the river Jordan, they were so afraid. Their response was to shut themselves securely in their walled city so that no one went out and no one came in. But the Lord had promised Joshua and his people that the city would be theirs. At Joshua's instructions, for six days the armed men followed by seven priests, blowing seven trumpets, leading the Ark of the Covenant, and lastly the rear guard, all circled the city once and then returned to their camp. On the seventh day they did the same, but this time marched round the city seven times. On the seventh time, Joshua told every man to shout – for the Lord would give them this city. So with the blast of the trumpets and the shout – the walls fell down and they went in and took the city (Joshua 6).

The Lord heralds His coming

The blowing of trumpets had a two-fold purpose: it heralded the coming of the Lord, but it also sounded an alarm for a coming battle (Joel 2:1). As the priest's trumpet blasts preceded the Ark of the Covenant, which was a symbol of the presence of the Lord, in the days of Joshua, so it will be when the Lord descends from heaven at His coming. He will come with a shout, with the voice of an archangel and with the trumpet of God (1 Thessalonians 4:16; compare Psalm 47:5;

Zephaniah 1:14-16; Matthew 24:30-31). As Joshua came with his army of men, so Christ will come with all His saints. As it says in Zechariah 14:5, "Thus the Lord my God will come and all the saints with You."

This will be the time for the Lord's judgement on the nations that set themselves up against God's people. Then the Lord will go forth and fight against those nations, as He fights in the day of battle (Zechariah 14:2-3). In the days of Joshua, God used him and His people to bring His judgement on some very wicked nations that had long passed God's forbearance – as He brought judgement on wicked Sodom and Gomorrah in the days of Abraham - and now the Lord settles His account at His coming.

Joshua saved those who helped God's people

Before their invasion of the land of Canaan, Joshua sent out two men to spy out the land, especially Jericho. When they came to Jericho they entered the city and came to the house of a harlot named Rahab and lodged there. It came to the ears of the king of Jericho that two men had entered the city whom they thought might be spies and had entered the house of Rahab. Therefore, the king sent to Rahab and demanded that these men be brought out. However, Rahab hid the men in her roof and deceived the king by saying they had already left the city before the night gate was closed – so she saved their lives.

Why did Rahab do this and risk her life for these men? Verses 9 to 11 of Joshua 2 explain why. She had heard of all that the Lord had done for His people at the Red Sea all those years ago, and how He had defended them against the two kings of the Armorites, at the other side of Jordan – Sihon and Og (Numbers 21:21-25, 31-35).

Then she made this declaration, "for the Lord your God – He is God in heaven above and earth beneath" (v.11). What a declaration of faith! And it was her faith that saved her and all her family when Israel took Jericho (Joshua 6:17; Hebrews 11:31).

The Lord will save those who help God's people

What God did for Rahab and her family in the days of Joshua, set a precedent for what will happen at the time of Christ's return, but this time on a national scale. Matthew 25: 31-46 speaks of the time when the Son of Man comes in all His glory, and all the holy angels with Him and when He sits on His throne of glory.

It continues to describe how all the nations will be gathered before Him, and He separates them one from another as a shepherd separates the sheep from goats – the sheep on the right hand and the goats on the left. Then He will say to them on the right hand, "Come you blessed of My Father, inherit the kingdom prepared for you from the foundation of the world."

Verses 35 and 36 describe why they have been chosen – but they ask, "When did we do these acts of kindness to you?" They are baffled, but the Lord says to them, "In as much as you did it to one of the least of my brethren, you did it to me." Therefore, the saved nations received the kingdom because they showed kindness to God's people.

Joshua leads his people to their inheritance

Gradually, little by little, Joshua led his people on into battle to take the land promised to them by the Lord. Joshua 11:23 says, "so Joshua took the whole land, according to all that the Lord had said to Moses, and Joshua gave it as an inheritance to Israel according to their divisions by their tribes. Then the land rested from war." Joshua chapters 13 to 21, describe the dividing and apportioning of the land to the tribes of Israel. Joshua 21:43-45 says:

> So the Lord gave to Israel all the land of which He had sworn to give to their fathers, and they took possession of it and dwelt in it. The Lord gave them rest all around, according to all that He had sworn to their fathers. And not a man of all their enemies stood against them; the Lord delivered all their enemies into their hand. Not a word failed of any good thing which the Lord had

spoken to the house of Israel. All came to pass.

Christ Jesus returns to take His people to their inheritance

Jesus said to His disciples, when the time came for Him to leave them;

> "Let not your heart be troubled, you believe in God, believe also in Me. In My Father's house are many mansions; if it were not so, I would have told you. I go to prepare a place for you. And if I go and prepare a place for you, I will come again and receive you to Myself; that where I am you may be also." (John 14:1-3)

All God's redeemed, who have put faith in God's provision for salvation, have been promised an inheritance in and with Christ. But as Christ explained, in His Father's house are many mansions, so our inheritances could differ. Some will dwell on the new earth (Matthew 5:5) and some in the new heavens – heavenly Jerusalem

(Hebrews 11:16; 12:22-24), and some in the heavenly places, far above all (Ephesians 1:11-14; 1:20-23; 2:4-6; Colossians 1:12; 3:1-4). At Christ's appearance and His coming, all will be brought into the inheritance promised to them to be ever with the Lord (1 Thessalonians 4:16-17; 1 Corinthians 15:22-23, 51-54).

DAVID
AND
SOLOMON

DAVID AND SOLOMON

To bring this booklet to a conclusion I am just going to briefly consider King David and King Solomon. There is so much which could be said about these two characters which would be a booklet in their own right. However, space does not permit this, but without them it would leave the purpose of God as portrayed in the Old Testament lacking and incomplete.

David – the anointed king

David, from out of all the sons of Jesse, was chosen by God to be king in place of Saul, who had been the people's choice and had failed through disobedience (1 Samuel 15). David was first anointed king of Judah at Hebron at the age of thirty, where he reigned for seven years (2 Samuel 2:4), and later king of all Israel (2 Samuel 5:3). He reigned in Jerusalem thirty three years making his total years as king, forty.

Jerusalem became known as the city of David. We could say David was a warrior king because he spent many of his years either fighting Saul, who had turned apostate, or fighting the Philistines who had taken over much of the land since the days of Joshua.

Eventually David had rest from all his enemies and this was when he had the desire to build a house for the Lord, for the Ark to rest in. Since the days of Moses, the Ark of the Covenant had had no resting dwelling place, since it resided only in the Tabernacle, a moveable tent. But the Lord, through Nathan the prophet, told him that he would not be the one to build Him a house, but one coming from his own loins, his son, would build the Lord a house to dwell in (2 Samuel 7:4-29).

Christ Jesus – the anointed King

Jesus Christ was born King of the Jews (Matthew 2: 2). He was welcomed into Jerusalem as a king (John 12:12-15), fulfilling prophecy from Zechariah 9:9, and He died with the title written above Him on the Cross which said, "JESUS OF NAZARETH, THE KING OF THE JEWS" (John 19:19). He was crowned with a crown of thorns.

Although He was God's anointed One (Isaiah 61:1; Acts 4:27), the Christ, He didn't take His seat on His throne and reign at His first advent, although He did at that time give a witness to, and a foretaste of, His kingly rule. First He must fulfil His role as the Servant king who came to give His life for the world.

However, at His Second Advent or coming, He will return as the warrior King and first deal with God's enemies. In Revelation 19, Christ is seen coming as the rider of a white horse, as the KING OF KINGS AND LORD OF LORDS. He comes clothed with His robe dipped in blood and a sharp sword proceeding out of His mouth, with which to strike the nations. He will take His seat, on His throne, and reign with a rod of iron until He has put all His enemies under His feet.

Solomon and his reign of peace

Following the death of King David, Solomon, his son by Bathsheba, reigned in his stead (1 Kings 2:12). Whilst the reign of David had been troubled with war, Solomon's rule was a reign of peace. 1 Kings 4: 24-25 says,

> For he had dominion over all the region on this side of the River from Tiphsah even to Gaza, namely over all the kings on this side of the River; and he had peace on every side all around him. And Judah and Israel dwelt safely, each man under his vine and his fig tree, from Dan as far as Beersheba, all the days of Solomon.

In answer to prayer, God gave Solomon wisdom and exceedingly great understanding and largeness of heart (1 Kings 4:29), and his fame spread far and wide. When the Queen of Sheba heard of Solomon's fame, she visited him at Jerusalem, and said,

"Blessed be the Lord your God, who delighted in you, setting you on the throne of Israel! Because the Lord has loved Israel forever, therefore He made you king, to do justice and righteousness." (1 Kings 10:9)

Whilst Solomon was blest with a reign of peace, he did make mistakes in the latter period of his life, highlighting the fact as mentioned in the introduction, that no man can emulate Christ in the fullest degree, because of sin.

Christ Jesus and His reign of peace

Christ's purpose in His return as the warrior King, is to first deal with all the enemies of God, in order that His rule of peace can begin.

The prophecy from Isaiah 11 speaks of the One who is the Rod from the stem of Jesse (the descendant of David), on whom the Spirit of the Lord rests. That is the Spirit of wisdom and understanding, the Spirit of counsel and might, and the Spirit of knowledge and of the fear of the Lord. He is the One who will rule with righteousness and equity, and as a result, all the earth shall be full of the knowledge of the Lord, as the waters cover the sea.

This will be the time when the people shall beat their swords into ploughshares and their spears into pruning hooks. When nation shall not lift up sword against nation and neither shall they learn war anymore (Isaiah 2:4). These are the latter days when everyone shall sit under his vine and under his fig tree, and no one shall make them afraid (Micah 4:1-5).

There are many, many more prophecies which describe the conditions that will prevail under Christ's reign of peace at His second coming, when the earth will be transformed back into the paradise at which it began in Eden, the garden of God.

MORE
ON CHRIST

MORE ON CHRIST

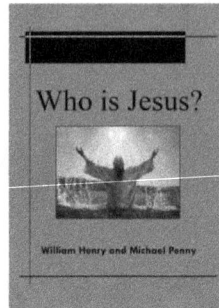

Jesus: God and Man
By Brian Sherring

The Manhood and Deity of Christ
By James Mead

Who is Jesus?
By William Henry and Michael Penny

For details of these books please visit

www.obt.org.uk

They can be ordered from that website or from:

The Open Bible Trust,
Fordland Mount, Upper Basildon,
Reading, RG8 8LU, UK.

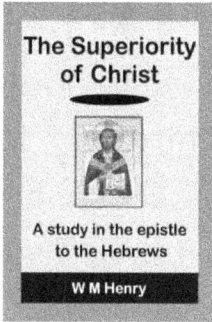

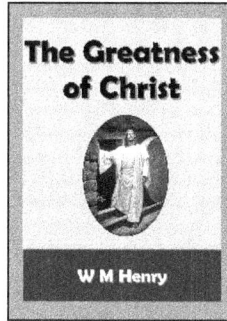

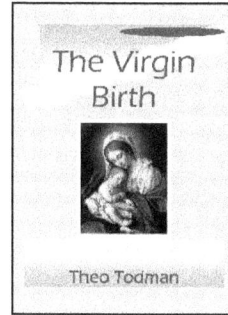

The Superiority of Christ
A study in the epistle to the Hebrews
By W M Henry

The Greatness of Christ
By W M Henry

The Virgin Birth
By Theo Todman

****

All these books are also available as eBooks
from Amazon and Apple
and as KDP paperbacks from Amazon.

ABOUT THE AUTHOR

Vicky Wilkinson was born in Hull, East Yorkshire, in 1945 and was educated at Sidmouth High School and Hull College of Commerce. She worked as a shorthand typist before marrying and having four sons. She then returned to the workforce carrying out secretarial services for a local firm in Hull, where she lives with her husband and now enjoys retirement.

Vicky Wilkinson was initially contacted by the Jehovah's Witnesses and was attracted to their position. However, through reading the Bible she came to see that salvation was by grace through faith in Jesus Christ, who was not 'a' god, but was 'the' God manifest in the flesh. She is a great advocate of the incarnation. Her story is told in her booklet *From Darkness to Glory*.

All her publications can be seen by visiting:

www.obt.org.uk/vicky-wilkinson

Search magazine

Vicky Wilkinson is a regular contributor to
Search magazine

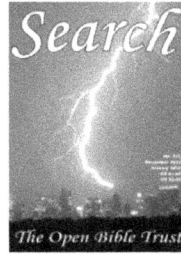

For a free sample of
The Open Bible Trust's magazine *Search*,
please email

admin@obt.org.uk

or visit

www.obt.org.uk/search

ALSO BY VICKY WILKINSON

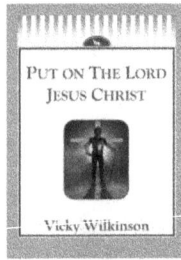

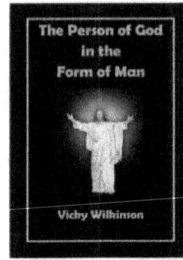

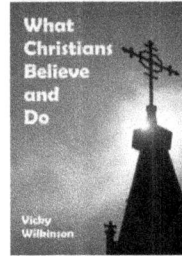

The Deity of Christ

Put on the Lord Jesus Christ

The Person of God in the Form of Man

To Walk in the Spirit

God's Work of Salvation

What Christians Believe and Do

Further details of these books can be seen on

www.obt.org.uk

They can be ordered from that website and from

The Open Bible Trust
Fordland Mount, Upper Basildon,
Reading RG8 8LU

They are also available as eBooks from
Amazon Kindle and Apple

and also as KDP paperbacks from Amazon.

ABOUT THIS BOOK

Cameos of Christ
in the lives of some
Old Testament Characters

Sometime ago, when attending a Bible study which looked into the lives of some of the Old Testament characters, the author was struck with the many cameos of Christ Jesus portrayed in their lives. What we have in this publication are six *Cameos of Christ* found in the lives of:

- Abraham and Joseph
- Moses and Joshua
- David and Solomon

www.ingramcontent.com/pod-product-compliance
Lightning Source LLC
Chambersburg PA
CBHW070540030426
42337CB00016B/2286